pylon
people

For Dafs,

You teach me to "SEE" God's extravagant beauty
and creativity in what seems ordinary.
That is what led me on this pylon adventure.
Best friend, love of my life, Wordsmith Wooly
May this "really seeing" in you continue to be part of
our gateway to divine creativity for HIS Glory.
#TeamWoolyAlways

Acknowledgments

Mam and Dad
Your bright eyes and wide hearts have shaped me beyond what I imagined. Two of my greatest gifts and treasures ever!

My sis Ali, Kev the Rev, Rob Lacey, Fawn, Paul Francis, Marie-Anne, and the SOW collective family – your love and passion for creativity, in different seasons have inspired my creative pursuit and upward gaze. Each of you uniquely taught me to think outside the box and to never underestimate the power of His breath through creative expression.

Lois – thank you for making everything you touch beautiful – and true to form – you made this offering beautiful!

pylon people

40 Days of Art and Meditations to Empower Your Spirit

CATH WOOLRIDGE

Illustrated by LOIS SECO

LION

Published by
Lion Hudson Limited
Wilkinson House, Jordan Hill Business Park
Banbury Road, Oxford OX2 8DR, England
www.lionhudson.com

ISBN 978 0 7459 8079 9

First edition 2020

Acknowledgments

Every effort has been made to trace copyright holders and to obtain permission for the use of copyright material. The publisher apologizes for any errors or omissions and would be grateful to be notified of any corrections that should be incorporated in future reprints of this book.

Scripture quotations marked TLB taken from The Holy Bible, Living Bible Edition, copyright © Tyndale House Publishers 1971. All rights reserved.

Scripture quotations marked NIV taken from the Holy Bible, New International Version Anglicised. Copyright © 1979, 1984, 2011 Biblica, formerly International Bible Society. Used by permission of Hodder & Stoughton Ltd, an Hachette UK company. All rights reserved. "NIV" is a registered trademark of Biblica. UK trademark number 1448790.

Scripture quotations marked NLT are taken from the Holy Bible, New Living Translation, copyright © 1996, 2004, 2015 by Tyndale House Foundation. Used by permission of Tyndale House Publishers, Inc., Carol Stream, Illinois 60188. All rights reserved. [revised 2019]

Scripture quotations marked ESV are from The Holy Bible, English Standard Version® (ESV®) copyright © 2001 by Crossway, a publishing ministry of Good News Publishers. All rights reserved.

Scripture quotations marked NKJV taken from the New King James Version. Copyright © 1982 by Thomas Nelson, Inc. Used by permission. All rights reserved.

Scripture excerpts marked NASB taken from the New American Bible with Revised New Testament, copyright © 1986, 1970 Confraternity of Christian Doctrine, Washington, D.C. and are used by permission of the copyright owner. All rights reserved. No part of the New American Bible may be reproduced in any form without permission in writing from the copyright owner.

Scripture quotations marked TPT are from The Passion Translation®. Copyright © 2017, 2018 by Passion & Fire Ministries, Inc. Used by permission. All rights reserved. ThePassionTranslation.com.

page 54-55 The Lord's Prayer as it appears in Common Worship: Services and Prayers for the Church of England (Church House Publishing, 2000) is copyright © The English Language Liturgical Consultation and is reproduced by permission of the publisher.

Page 109 Just One Touch From the King – Godfrey BirtillCopyright © 2006 Thankyou Music (Adm. by CapitolCMGPublishing.com excl. UK & Europe, adm. by Integrity Music, part of the David C Cook family, songs@integritymusic.com)

A catalogue record for this book is available from the British Library

Printed and bound in China, July 2020, LH54

CONTENTS

Pylon People are powered people;
Praying people;
Present people;
Perspective people;
Pregnant-with-passion people;
A population of persons prone to point to papa's path.
Pylon People are not pipe-dream people,
But propel into Promised-Land purpose.
Pointing up,
Peering up to papa of all planets.
A people in pursuit of him perpetually.
Pylon People praise him 'cos they've pinpointed love in person.
He parted from papa of planets to pay for our painful predicament,
Planning a prospective of peace, purity, and perfect protection.
Pylon People are presence-potent people,
Pledging their purpose and potential to pursuing the Prince of Peace.
A posture of present,
A posture of all welcome at all times.
Pylon People are a prophetic people,
Promotion perspectives of pauper to princess,
Poor to prized, paralyzed to powerful.
Pylon People are powered people,
Powered by the protagonist of all history and destiny.

Introduction

I believe God is awakening a generation of Pylon People. Pylons are powered, and I believe God wants to empower a people who know their identity in Christ and live extravagantly for him – empowered by his spirit. Pylons stand with arms open wide. Father, help us to welcome the last, least, and the lost, always. Pylons stand tall, almost giving the illusion that they are touching heaven, yet are rooted in the earth. Pylon People are a generation that look up, but extend the upward encounter to an outward generosity – touching heaven, changing earth. Pylons are often misunderstood; they stand out, seemingly counter to the culture of countryside civilization. We too as Pylon People may sometimes stand out as different, counter-cultural, living in the world, but not "of" it.

Pylons stand in line, attached one to another by powered lines – a pylon army. We too need to attach ourselves to other Pylon People – standing as an army, lining every community with prayer, praise, love, generosity, and grace. Where there is unity, God commands a blessing. We are all in this together!

Pylons simply stand while the power does the work. We are called to stand available while the All-Powerful One acts in our surrender. Pylons survive and thrive in summer and winter months, in springtime or autumn. Pylons are in it for the long haul. Pylons carry lines of communication. The sons and daughters must say and do what they see their Father do, communicators of mercy and justice. A revolution of Pylon People is arising. I want to be one. Maybe you do too.

Through the powered days, the powerless days, the rainy seasons, the sunny months, join us in a pylon pilgrimage as we unpack, connect, and move forward through the next forty days.

How to Use this Book

I am so excited for you to engage your heart, mind, and creativity with this book over the next forty days. Part One allows you space to get into the rhythm of applying creativity. Parts Two to Four go into the devotion in more detail, whilst also giving you creative and meditative responses for each day.

We are all creative, and these forty days are for your personal expressions of creativity. Be brave. Practise wonder. One of my favourite quotes, attributed to Winston Churchill says, "Success is not final, failure is not fatal: it is the courage to continue that counts." Creativity takes courage. Be curious. Be kind to yourself. Be willing. Put busyness aside and give yourself to the pull of your creativity. Watch as you come alive.

If you feel a knot in your belly because there is a dissonance between your daily reality and your dreams, do one thing: don't let the moment pass. Dig a little deeper and discover the beauty of creativity. You will be amazed!

Sketchnoting

In this book I use the word "sketchnoting" as a creative prompt for you. This is simply the idea of taking notes through sketching. It can be a single word that has a lot of other words or phrases around it to help "unpack" it (see example), or it could be a drawing to help communicate what God is saying to you. I want this journal and journey to be unique to you, so don't get stuck on the prompts. This is your journey.

I have also included suggestions for further meditation, which can be used alongside the creative responses or on their own.

PART ONE

DAYS 1–10

Pylon People are Powered People

As Powered People, we need to be connected to the source, otherwise we are just powerless eyesores in the landscape of life.

In the next ten days we will unpack and discover what it is to be constantly connected to the ultimate power source that is our Father in heaven. He is not just our far-away Father, up in the sky, but our every-single-day dad from whom we get our original DNA.

An Invitation

> *His unchanging plan has always been to adopt us into his own family by sending Jesus Christ to die for us. And he did this because he wanted to!* **Ephesians 1:5 (TLB)**
>
> *Oh, the depth of the riches of the wisdom and knowledge of God!* **Romans 11:33 (NIV)**

Are you treading shallow waters, but ache for the depths?

The trouble with shallow waters is the gathering of floating fears at our feet, and the dregs of past realities consuming our gaze, distorting our perspectives, and hindering us from stepping out.

The deep waters are the place where fears drown under the weight and vast expanse of Love himself; a place where we abandon the pattern of our own breathing to the rhythm of his. A place where we are caught up in the current that draws us to the depths of the Father.

Read the poem opposite and use it as a prayer to commit to stepping into the depths with our heavenly papa over the next forty days.

The Deep

This "shallow end" survival
Comfortable
Content
Surviving in the shallow waters
My soul's "deep" hurtling to a descent
This shallow
Is hollow
NO substance
I was not made to be an empty vessel
That when shaken, the world's lusts are all that
  are heard in this shell that's now me
Surviving in the shallow
I was not made for here

The diving board hovers aloof in my periphery
Surely not up there?
I mean it's risky, right,
Deep waters?
What if I can't catch my breath?
Then my mind skips a beat remembering this
"Survival" feels more and more
Like death to my bones
I was not made for here

So the peripheral view of that aloof diving board
Now becomes my reality
My new peripheral seems somewhat too far
  down for my liking

The shallow waters beckon,
But then "surviving" recollections soon
  hush
Those shallows beckon
"But what if I can't catch my breath?"
What then?

My soul's deep whispers subliminally
"You were not made to survive – you were made to live."
What kind of an answer is that?
I repeat, as the sweat literally drips off my forehead
But what if I can't catch my...
"Survival" I was not made to survive
– I was made to live
I jumped!

Hurtling through the air
Not knowing the result of what now feels like
  the dumbest of decisions
My mind on repeat:
What have I done?
What have I done?
What if I can't catch my...

I hit the water
Now deep under
Completely immersed
My flesh may not be able to catch its
  breath –
Yet the moment I hit the water my soul's
  deep took its first breath in what seemed
  like for ever

Survival obliterated
Life in its seedling beginnings
I was made for here
I was made for the deep.

Creative Response

Take a moment... will you dive in?
Reread the poem and then annotate it with words, highlights, symbols, images, and pictures. What stands out? Let the Holy Spirit highlight words or phrases to you.

Meditative Moment

With Holy-Spirit-inspired imagination, picture yourself deep in water. Just as you are about to expire, you unexpectedly find you are able to breathe freely under water like a fish. What does God want to say to you at the beginning of this adventure of being deeply connected to him?

Orphans to Sons

> *The Spirit you received does not make you slaves, so that you live in fear again; rather, the spirit you received brought about your adoption to sonship. And by him we cry, "Abba, Father".*
> **Romans 8:15 (NIV)**

> *I will not abandon you as orphans - I will come to you.*
> **John 14:18 (NLT)**

Sometimes we live out of the spirit of an orphan, when in reality we have the freedom to live in the spirit of sonship. Let's look at some examples of how "orphans" behave and how "sons" (and "daughters") behave.

Orphans may be bound and motivated by fear. Sons are fuelled by love. Orphans may strive for praise, acceptance, and approval of man. Sons know they are totally accepted in God's love and justified by his grace. Orphans are defined by what they do. Sons are defined by what God has done and *who they are.* Orphans may use their gifts to climb the ladder of success. Sons use their gifts to climb into their Father's arms. Orphans see God as Master. Sons see God as Father.

Creative Response

Ask the Holy Spirit for a word or an image of who you are as a son or daughter. Take time to sketch this word or image, make it beautiful in your own way, let it seep into you, annotate it, meditate on it. *You are a child of God!*

Meditative Moment

Picture Jesus taking any labels of unacceptance from you and burning them with glee. With great pride he positions you for the family photograph. How does this feel?

As a child of the most high, you carry his name and his inheritance. All that he has is yours. Pick a place of great scarcity in your life, and then picture the Father reframing that picture with his abundance.

Change Your Mind

> *Let God transform you into a new person by changing the way you think.* **Romans 12:2 (NLT)**
>
> *See what great love the Father has lavished on us, that we should be called children of God! And that is what we are! The reason the world does not know us is that it did not know him.*
> **1 John 3:1 (NIV)**

For some of us it's difficult to grasp what it means to be a son or daughter. Perhaps we are basing our perception of who God is or who we are on past experiences, and out of those life experiences we have "made up our minds". So, we need to have our minds changed. Pay attention to some of the thoughts that go through your mind when you think of God as Father, or when you think of yourself as a son or daughter. What are those thoughts? Are they lies? Do they line up with what the Bible says about who God is and who you are? We need to take those thoughts captive and replace them with truth. We need to recycle and dispose of our debilitating mind modes.

God is always in the business of recycling. Making the old, new. He is the God of the divine exchange – taking ashes and exchanging them for beauty. All despair can be replaced for hope; all fear for exceptional strength! This is our God!

Creative Response

Below is a page from my creative journal. I drew this process to help me recycle old thoughts I had about myself and put them through the "new mind skin" in light of God's word to create new thoughts about myself.

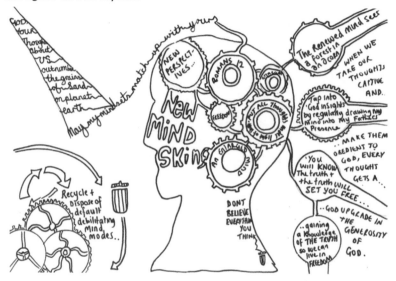

Take a thought that you have identified; ask the Holy Spirit to show you God's truth. Take the old thought and recycle it through the healing process of God's love. What is the new thought? Using the outline on the following page, do the same with your old thought.

Meditative Moment

Ask the Holy Spirit to identity a negative emotion you feel consistently. Then ask him to reframe that moment. (Perhaps, as a child, you had to wait a long time to be picked up by a parent, making you feel as though you weren't worthy of being remembered.) The Holy Spirit might re-frame that moment.

Without Measure
Measure it with Calvary

> *As far as the east is from the west, SO far has he removed our transgressions from us.* **Psalm 103:12 (NIV, emphasis mine)**

> *And I pray that you... may have power... to grasp how wide and long and high and deep is the love of Christ, and to know this love that surpasses knowledge – that you may be filled to the measure of all the fullness of God.* **Ephesians 3:17–19 (NIV)**

Because of the cross, he can do immeasurably more than we could ever dare to ask or imagine. Because of the cross, we get his spirit without measure. Because of the cross, there is no measure to his forgiveness. Because of the cross we always measure up. Because of Jesus.

Creative Response

We are completely free! On the following page, doodle, write, or draw the things that you have been measuring by worldly standards that now need to come under the measurement of Calvary. Ask Jesus to show you how he measures your life, value, worth and his love for you.

Meditative Moment

Picture a compass over the galaxies and then picture beyond the known universe. See your sin, your guilt, your fear, your shame thrown outside the galaxies, outside time... eradicated. Imagine you have an unlimited bank balance of mercy, wisdom, and love. No matter how many withdrawals you make, your funds are never depleted. How would you live if you believed this true reality?

Measure it with calvary

Jesus, the Son, Revealing the Father

> *You are my Son, whom I love; with you I am well pleased.*
> **Mark 1:11 (NIV)**

> *And he will be called Wonderful Counsellor, Mighty God, Everlasting Father, Prince of Peace.* **Isaiah 9:6 (NIV)**

Jesus' mission was to bring us to the Father, and to reveal to us what the Father is like. He said that the "Son can do... only what he sees his Father doing" (John 5:19, NIV). He is the original son who knows exactly what the Father is like when it comes to the subject of sonship.

When we look at the story of the Prodigal Son in Luke 15:11–32, we see that there are actually three sons in the parable: the son who left, the son who stayed home, and the Son (Jesus) who's telling the story.

So, we can fully trust that the response of the father in the story is the true character and response of our Father in heaven.

Creative Response

Read the story of the Prodigal Son. Ask the
Holy Spirit to reveal something new to you in the
story. Sketch any words or ideas that come up.
Spend time contemplating Jesus' mission to bring us to
the Father and what that means to you. Feel free to take
this time to colour in the word art as you pray and ponder
through this.

Meditative Moment

Search for images of the Prodigal Son online. Linger on the one that
appeals to you. Ask the Holy Spirit to place you in the emotional
core of this story.

Flying Free

Now the Lord is the spirit, and where the spirit of the Lord is, there is freedom. **2 Corinthians 3:17 (NIV)**

So Christ has truly set us free. Now make sure you stay free.
Galatians 5:1 (NLT)

So often we settle for the safety of the birdcage when, in reality, the door is wide open and we were made to fly free. We assume that our protective surroundings define our freedom because our captivity has become the safe place. But there is so much more. We need to redefine and live in the sort of freedom Christ died and rose again for. This freedom lies beyond the open door and in the wide, open spaces of his unquenchable love. It is the spacious life that is the free life. It is the spacious life that is the real brand of "protected".

There is freedom waiting for you,
On the breezes of the sky,
And you ask
"What if I fall?"
Oh but my darling,
What if you fly?
Erin Hanson

Celebrate risk as much as success. Failure refines us.

Creative Response

Within the bars and the base of the birdcage on the following page, identify some of the things that are keeping you captive. Write some words. Draw a path of flight with your words to freedom.

Meditative Moment

What is your greatest fear about moving from the birdcage of the known boundaries to the unlimited sky of freedom? Ask Jesus to speak to you about your fear. Is it true that if you knew he loved you perfectly, you would not fear?

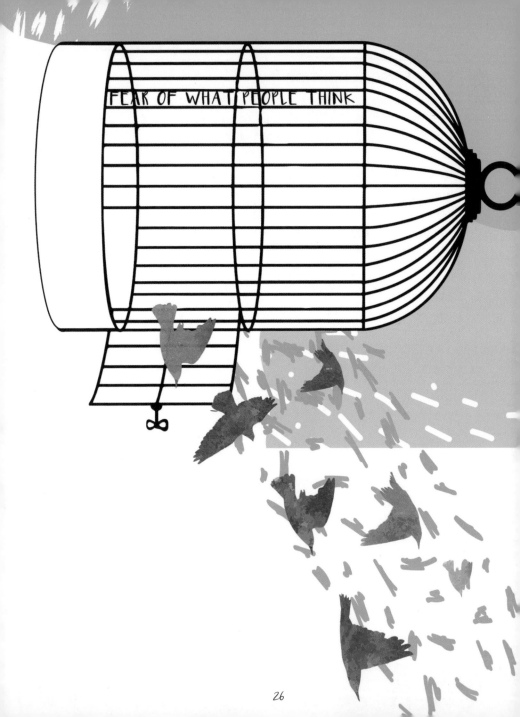

Known

> But now... O Israel, the one who formed you says, "Do not be afraid, for I have ransomed you. I have called you by name; you are mine."
> **Isaiah 43:1 (NLT)**

> O Lord, you have examined my heart and know everything about me. **Psalm 139:1 (NLT)**

In a world of 7 billion people, it's easy to feel lost in a crowd. But you are seen. You are completely known; from your triumphs to your trials, from your mess to your most magnificent moments – you are completely known and completely loved.

You are not owned like a new car. You are connected like a new bride. You are not a number in a population, but a uniquely known son or daughter. You are not God's trophy, but actually his greatest treasure. He loves you at your worst moment as much as he does at your best. He knows everything about you and celebrates all that you are.

Creative Response

Sketchnote your name, asking God what he loves about you and how he uniquely created you. Spend time really diving deep into your identity: the things that make you *you*. *He knows you and he sees you.*

Meditative Moment

Ask the Holy Spirit to tell you your true kingdom identity, the name God joyfully calls you in this present season.
How does it feel to be known and completely loved? What does this feeling do to your fears?

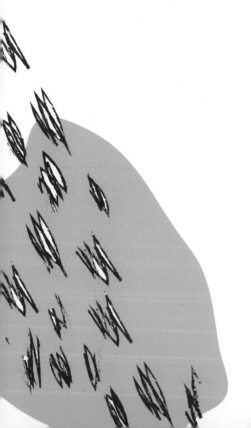

Earthed Pylons

> *My response is to get down on my knees before the Father, this*
> *magnificent Father who parcels out all heaven and earth. I ask*
> *him to strengthen you by his spirit – not a brute strength but a*
> *glorious inner strength – that Christ will live in you as you open*
> *the door and invite him in. And I ask him that with both feet*
> *planted firmly on love, you'll be able to take in with all followers*
> *of Jesus the extravagant dimensions of Christ's love. Reach out*
> *and experience the breadth! Test its length! Plumb the depths!*
> *Rise to the heights! Live full lives, full in the fullness of God.*
> **Ephesians 3:14–19 (MSG)**

The wires between pylons carry electricity, but this electricity can't be used unless it has been earthed. Ephesians 3 talks of us being earthed and grounded in God's love in order to live the fullest life. Just as pylons are consistently and constantly connected to electricity, we have the opportunity and ability to choose to be in a constant deep connection with God. Through earthing our identity in his love every single day, and in navigating through all of life's moments, aware of his power at work in us, we are connected. Pylon People are connected people!

Creative Response

On the following page, draw your own pylon. Think about how you can stay connected – not just in your God-time, but in the rhythms of the day: the school run, the receiving of bad news, the stressful moments, and the stress-free moments.

Meditative Moment

Have you ever met someone who is "grounded in God's love"? What struck you about that person? Earthing our identity in his love requires intentionality. Read Jude 1:24 and ask the Holy Spirit for some ways you can intentionally keep yourself in the love of God.

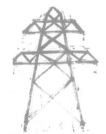

Pylon People are Powered People

> *Now to him who is able to do immeasurably more than all we ask or imagine, according to his power that is at work within us...*
> **Ephesians 3:20 (NIV)**

As sons and daughters we carry the power and authority of the Father. As Jesus only did what he saw the Father doing, by being powered and connected, we can do the same and bring the kingdom, our home, here on earth.

Being a powered pylon person, means choosing:

- The deep over the shallow.
- Being a son or daughter instead of an orphan.
- New starting places for our mindsets.
- To recognize that his love is without measure.
- To allow Jesus to reveal the Father to us, flying free, living the revelation of being completely known and completely loved, and being rooted and established in his love.

You have been uniquely made and were created for deep connection.

Creative Response

Spend some time today focusing on your level of connection. Maybe just sit in silence, pray, worship, go for a walk, ponder until you are in wonder. Actively connect!

Meditative Moment

If God can do more than you can imagine, might your ideas of your future be too small?

With the potential of being powered and connected to the source of all power and authority, could you possibly be operating at too low an amperage? Listen intentionally to the Holy Spirit as he inspires you to greater power. Where might be a specific place you could carry his immeasurable love and power?

Connection

Reflect over the past 9 days. Use the pylons below to connect and express your revelations from each day in words, images, or collaging. Think seriously about some of the questions you have. Ask the Holy Spirit to fill in the gaps – you are on a journey and he has *all* the answers.

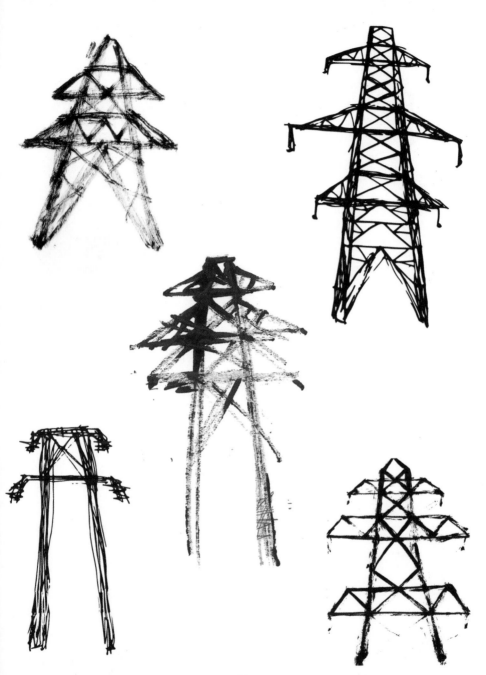

PART TWO

DAYS 11–20

Pylon People are Praying People

As praying people, we are privileged to experience God through conversation and contemplation. As praying people, we recognize that prayer isn't a boring monologue droning on and on.

Joy Dawson says, "If you've ever been to a dull prayer meeting, God wasn't given the opportunity to be in charge!"[1]

We stop and listen to the incredible voice of God. We are in a conversation with the God of the universe – prayer is a two-way conversation between you and, as Max Lucado puts it, the "God [who] would rather die than live without you."[2]

All love, all wisdom, awaits you on this journey of discovery.

Welcome to this ten-day adventure in creative ways of conversing and listening to God in prayer!

1   Joy Dawson, *How to Pray for Someone Near You Who is Away from God* (Edmonds, WA: YWAM Publishing, 1999).

2   Max Lucado, *Grace for the Moment* (Nashville, TN: Thomas Nelson, 2007).

24/7 Prayer

> *Rejoice always, pray without ceasing, give thanks in all circumstances; for this is the will of God in Christ Jesus for you.*
> **1 Thessalonians 5:16–18 (ESV)**

This concept of "praying without ceasing" can seem like an impossible task. You might feel doomed to failure before you even begin. However, I have good news for you! Our heavenly Father is not far away, waiting to be impressed by our constancy in praying. He is near and *constantly* pursuing us... in every moment, and every breath. When we make ourselves present to him, we find him waiting for us with joy.

Life is one hectic distraction but the command to "pray without ceasing" is for our good, not because God wants to lord it over us with impossible demands. God's commands are always for our freedom, and this open highway of conversation, listening, and communing with him is like treasure when we become awake to it.

I created a simple creative prayer map using alliteration to help me remember how to focus my prayers on the days of the week. This means that when I am driving or walking from one meeting to another, cooking, or the like, I can bring to mind the day and engage with praying without ceasing.

- **Marriage Monday**: Prayers for my marriage and the marriages around me.
- **Transforming Tuesday**: Prayers for the people in my life who don't yet know the almighty God of love.
- **Wales and the World Wednesday**: Prayers for my nation Wales, and the needs of the world.
- **Thank-You Thursday**: Breath prayers of thanks like a constant flowing fountain from my heart to my papa.

- **Family-and-Friends Friday**: Prayers specifically bringing the needs and loves of my family and pals to the God who is sovereign over all.
- **STOP, LOOK, and LISTEN Saturday and Sunday:** No agenda other than that – I will *stop*, engage my heart with *his*; I will *look* up until my gaze finds his eyes amid all the eyes and voices that try to grab my attention, and I will *listen* – then out of the overflow of these beautiful moments, offer prayers in response.

Creative Response

Use the calendar to creatively map out a mind map for your "praying without ceasing" week. Memorize it and get praying.

Meditative Moment

How would my life be different if I truly believed God is constantly, joyfully pursuing me? What would need to change for my prayer life to go from a monologue of requests to a surprising and unexpected conversation with God?

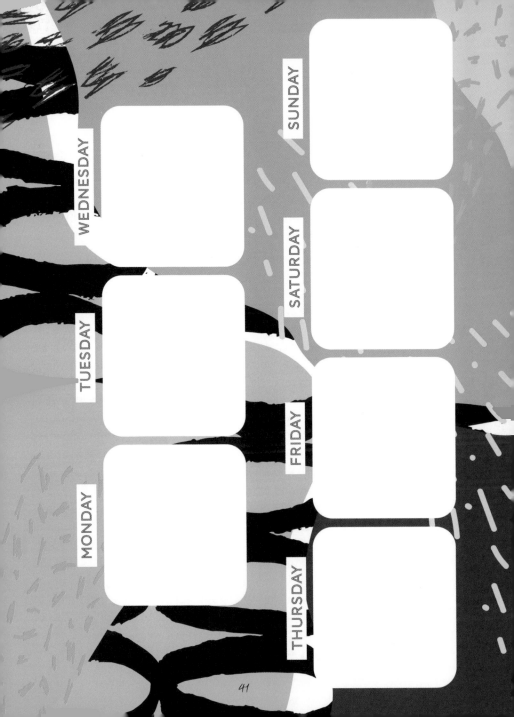

MONDAY

TUESDAY

WEDNESDAY

THURSDAY

FRIDAY

SATURDAY

SUNDAY

Face Seeking, Not Shadow Seeking

> *The one thing I ask of the Lord – the thing I seek most – is to live in the house of the Lord all the days of my life, delighting in the Lord's perfections and meditating in his Temple.* **Psalm 27:4 (NLT)**

> *Look to the Lord and his strength; seek his face always.* **Psalm 105:4 (NIV)**

In Psalm 91, the psalmist describes dwelling in the secret place of the most high, abiding under the shadow of the almighty, saying, "He is my refuge and my fortress; my God, in him I will trust" (verse 2, NKJV). He goes on to say, "He shall cover you with his feathers, and under his wings you shall take refuge" (verse 4, NKJV).

Dwelling in God's shadow is a place of proximity and security. It is easy to scurry to a place under his shadow. It is a refuge. Wonderfully, we are invited to more. We are privileged not only to abide under his shadow, but to lift our eyes and live face-to-face in *intimacy*. Prayer is a means by which we can dwell both in the shadow of the almighty but also gaze upon him in abandon and intimacy.

Pylon People are praying people who don't just settle for the shadow of their God, but pursue the intimacy of prayer by gazing continually upon him. Imagine the scene: you are out for a meal in your favourite restaurant; you want to be there on a "table for two" basis with God in the seat opposite.

This is an opportunity for you to engage fully in gazing upon him, to hear him speak truth over you, to share laughter over the funny stories of the day, and maybe share a handkerchief moment when you reveal some of the deep pains of your heart.

But as you arrive at the restaurant, you remove God from the seat opposite and replace him with your worries and fears. God then gets demoted to the waiter in your story.

He is now the one to whom you give your orders and make complaints. He isn't an intimate participant in the conversation any more. You are now more intimately acquainted with the worries and fears of the day, which sit in the place of honour opposite you.

Pylon People are people who desire to seek the fullness of his face in prayer. They want to keep God directly opposite as a beloved, engaging friend rather than as a figure on the periphery.

Creative Response

We often use the prayer room as a classroom to learn, a boardroom to do business with God, or a war room to develop strategies to fight. These are all well and good, but first and foremost prayer should be a *living room* for intimate interaction with the Father.

On the next page is an illustration of two armchairs and speech bubbles. After a time of reflection, what would you would find yourself saying to God today? Write it in one of the speech bubbles. Wait a while and listen, then write out his response to the deep prayers of your heart in the speech bubble from the opposite armchair.

Meditative Moment

What might I experience if I intentionally gaze at the face of God for three minutes, silently right now?

Do I see in his eyes the love he has for me? Why or why not?

Climb High

> *He carried me away... to a mountain great and high.*
> **Revelation 21:10 (NIV)**

In the swirl of so many ideologies contending for our allegiance, as praying Pylon People, can we embrace God's higher thoughts of truth?

As followers of Jesus, we are invited to pray from a *high* view. Scripture says that his thoughts and ways are "higher" than ours. This higher view comes from living by *faith* and not sight. Pylon People are a praying people who pray in faith according to the ways and thoughts of Jesus. Think about it: only when we stand high do we see far. Broad landscapes cannot be truly seen from the lowlands.

Just as we see best at higher altitudes in the natural world, we see the Father best from the spiritual heights. In the scripture above, when John was shown the new Jerusalem descending out of heaven, he was carried away to a "mountain great and high". Just before this, he had seen a seashore and a "beast" rising up from the deep (Revelation 13:1).

Sometimes our prayers are too focused on the "beasts" in this modern world and we don't look in faith for the "New Jerusalems" coming out of the sky. Our prayers dwell at sea level and don't take flight to new heights of faith. Jesus lovers are meant to have the mountain view, the long view, the wide view, the "deep understanding" view. This comes from times of prayer where we:

1. Shut the door of distraction to enjoy time alone with Jesus.
2. Gaze on his ultimate victory, his finished work.
3. Pray through the eyes of the Holy Spirit from the high viewpoint of God's holy ambitions.

How do we keep that high altitude vision in our lives?

We must live on the bread of Scripture. No matter how good your local bakery is, it's the best donut in town! Scripture gives us language in prayer, and guards our hearts against tolerating ways that may grieve the Holy Spirit.

Climb high and look through the eyes of Jesus to get perspective beyond our present circumstances in the lowlands.

Creative Response

I love high, wide, long, beautiful views. I live in a valley in Wales, and I have a high place just above my gorgeous valley where I go to pray most days – the high secret place! Why not get outside to a high point near you? It could be the highest point in your garden, the mountain in your neighbourhood, or you could even draw a high view that you have been to and inspires you. Engage with your heavenly Father in prayer conversation and ask him simply to show you some of his "higher thoughts".

Opposite is a photograph of a high place in Nazareth, the town where Jesus lived. I imagine him doing the same thing as us right now – climbing a high place to pray and see a new perspective. Using a photograph you print out or on a picture you have drawn, or even on the wide landscape picture opposite, hang the "higher thoughts" like stars amidst the image. Pray into each one and see faith arise as we catch the higher thought prayers of a heavenly Father who sees way beyond the natural.

Meditative Moment

Picture yourself at the top of the highest building in your city or region; what is remarkable to you? Picture yourself standing with Jesus overlooking Jerusalem as he says, "Oh Jerusalem, how often I would have gathered you, but you would not!" (based on Matthew 23:37). What are your emotions as you stand with him?

climb

Signpost Your Life

Devote yourselves to prayer, being watchful and thankful.
Colossians 4:2 (NIV)

I love signs! But I often have to be watchful in order to catch them. When I travel to a new location, I need to be watchful for the signs so I get to the desired destination. When I follow them accurately, I am most thankful!

I also *love* shabby chic statement signs; they are *all* over my house. When I read them, my soul gets lavishly filled with truth that connects me to *the way, the truth, and the life*. I need to be watchful in order to catch these, as they can so easily slip from my view as I get distracted in the hustle and bustle of the day.

When I'm watchful and see them as I enter and leave my house, I am so much more thankful and prayer flows! Some examples of signs in my house are:

"Scatter kindness";
"Bless this house with love and laughter";
"Be your own kind of beautiful";
"I am a child of God";
"I will never leave you".

Psalm 119:29 says, "Barricade the road that goes nowhere... I choose the true road to somewhere, I post your road signs at every curve and corner. I... cling to whatever you tell me" (MSG).

As Pylon People, we should signpost our lives so we are reminded of who God is and who we are, and how we should live in response to his great love.

Creative Response

Look at the empty signposts on the following page and pause your heart. Engage with heaven and write in these signposts to his somewhere – a simple few words that are relevant and significant to your life right now, as you seek his perfect ways. Ask the God who knows you better than you know yourself to signpost your life. Add your own signposts if you need or want to. If you have a bit more time, why not make these into signs and stick them up to catch your eye around your house/office/bedroom/medicine cabinet mirror/car dashboard?

Meditative Moment

Picture God writing signs to his heart specifically for you; what do they say? Picture writing signposts to people you love who have yet to meet Jesus. What do they say?

Transfigured Prayer

As he prayed, the appearance of his face was altered.
Luke 9:29 (NKJV)

When we look over the life of Jesus on earth, we see so many beautiful things he did for love. Observe with me the seven events which stand out like the pinnacles of a mountain. These are: his birth, his baptism, his temptation, his transfiguration, his crucifixion, his resurrection, his ascension.

Today we look at Jesus' transfiguration as a towering peak pregnant with significance. Notice three small words **"as he prayed..."** We are resolutely told that Jesus goes up the mountain to pray and that his transfiguration happened "as he prayed". As image bearers of God, what happened to Jesus may happen in ourselves spiritually, progressively, gradually if we engage prayfully in his presence. As praying Pylon People, our appearance changes as we spend time with the Father in prayer. God needs our knees before our hands. We need more knee-mail than email. Real prayer is like an ascending of the soul to a summit where we meet peace and love himself.

A high altitude transforms our view of a landscape, as does prayer in the spiritual world. When you climb to a mountain height, you see the relative size and importance of things in a way you never could have from below. We can begin to determine between the *seemingly* great and the *truly* great.

Many of the concerns that seemed huge at ground level shrink into insignificance as we see them against the really *big* things.

Let's fight for the God's-eye-view! In that secret trust of communion with the eternal we can be lifted up above the world in which we mix and move. Only then can we begin to see things as they appear to the eye of heaven itself.

Creative Response

On the page opposite are two mounatins with the headings "Worldly ambitions" and "Heavenly ambitions". Write out the worldly ambitions in your heart; spend time praying into them, and see what God says about them. Some will remain, I'm sure; write them over in the "heavenly ambition" mountain side as you hear. Some false ambitions might be rectified. But just wait for God and see your ambitions, plans, worries, dreams, sorrows, cares fall into their true proportion as you keep climbing that mountain for *his* high view. His high view is always going to be the *best* view! The climb is worth it.

Meditative Moment

Have you ever witnessed someone transfigured by prayer? How did you feel as you observed them? Imagine being present watching Jesus transfigured before you. What emotions are you feeling?

HEAVENLY AMBITIONS

WORLDLY AMBITIONS

Taught and Caught

Lord, teach us to pray. **Luke 11:1 (NIV)**

Pylons *stand* as silent sentinels in the landscapes all around us. They may seem like useless eyesores, but it is their posture of simply *standing* that allows them to function effectively. They stand "available", allowing the electricity to run through them to homes across the country.

Pylon People's greatest ability is our *avail*ability to the love and power of God flowing through us. As we stand in surrender, he is given the space to breathe within us. As we stand in surrender, his strength is made perfect. In our surrender, he speaks.

In this surrender his power is at work *in us;* it even teaches us to pray when we don't know how.

In Luke, we are given the Lord's Prayer, which is a direct response to Jesus' disciples asking him, "Lord, teach us to pray."

Just a few weeks ago, I was feeling rattled and weary and couldn't get my head or heart in the zone of prayer. I asked God, just like my brothers in Scripture, *"Lord, teach me to pray today."* The memory of reciting the Lord's Prayer in school assemblies came to mind, so I got my journal and wrote out the Lord's Prayer and in each line, I saw a different "key" to opening up my heart to prayerful overflow.

Scripture gives us a powerful vocabulary and wise mentorship in prayer.

> *Our Father* – PERSON. He is ABBA, our Father. We are his sons and daughters. He is near and close not far off.
>
> *in heaven*
>
> *hallowed be your name* – POSITION. He and his ways are higher than ours. He is sovereign.
>
> *your kingdom come* – PRE-EMINENCE. His kingdom is supreme to any other; it holds number one position in the order of all.

your will be done – PURPOSE. His will is the best way. He holds the master map over all our lives and he desires his purpose in our lives for he loves and wants the best for us.

on earth as it is in heaven – PATTERN. His desire is to see the beauty of the patterns of heaven displayed on earth.

Give us today our daily bread – PROVISION. His bread is the best we could ever eat. ALL we need is found in him.

And forgive us our sins – PARDON. The finished work of Christ allows us to be washed white in the epic flow of his everyday new mercies won and established at the cross.

As we forgive those who sin against us – PURITY. That we would learn the PURE heart of God, even when we are hurt.

And lead us not into temptation, but deliver us from evil – PROTECTION. He is our wrap-around shield.

For yours is the kingdom, the power, and the glory – POWER. He is capable of accomplishing infinitely more than we could dare ask or imagine.

For ever and ever – PERMANENT. Nothing can take away or compare to the promise we have in him.

Amen

True prayer is a way of life, not just an emergency call when tragedy strikes.

Creative Response

In this beautiful, strategic prayer that is given to us by Jesus himself, take all the noted P's, on the following page, and write or draw around them, unpacking your heart as you think of these keys of promise, then pray it with all your thoughts added in!

Meditative Moment

Simply pray the Lord's Prayer aloud. Slowly recite it and let it truly sink in.

person postion

pre-eminence

purpose pattern

provision pardon

purity protection

power

permanent

Word Wielding

> *Take... the sword of the spirit, which is the word of God.*
> **Ephesians 6:17 (NIV)**

Pylon People position themselves to surrender to the work, ways, and words of God, powerfully at work within them. The electricity that runs through pylons is much like the unstoppable current of God's love and power running through us.

As we explored yesterday, sometimes we may not know how to pray or what to pray, especially in dark or difficult seasons. How do we keep connected to prayer, our direct line to heaven, when the storms come to disrupt our lines of communication? Praying his word has been a lifesaver for me in such moments.

In Ephesians 6 we are told about armour and weapons that are available to us in Jesus. The armour protects us, safeguarding us against the accuser. The sword is his word, which we use to *fight* the lies and fears which often bombard our minds and hearts. Pylons stand with arms outstretched, reminiscent of a soldier with a sword in each hand. In the moments when we feel lost or assailed, we only have to remember the armour and weapons of his word, with which he equips us.

Let's pray by wielding the word in the face of opposition, demolishing and cutting into pieces the lies of the enemy with the promises of scripture. Just last week, when my heart and mind reeled with insecurity, I picked up his word and opened it to Jehosophat's prayer, which simply says, "We do not know what to do, but our eyes are on you" (2 Chronicles 20:12, NIV).

I decided to use this as a prayer of *faith* in a moment of fear. I started repeatedly declaring and praying it aloud, wielding the sword of his word in the face of opposition.

At first it felt hopeless, but as I continued to pray in faith, and not in sight – this one line of promise directly from my brother Jehosophat's mouth – I started casting out that fear. Fear-driven thoughts were replaced with power, love, and a sound mind.

God wants to inhabit our prayers. As Pylon People we stand surrendered, with a sword in each hand, ready to pack the best punch with his perfect promises.

Destructive regimes that seek to destroy you can be dismantled *right now* through wielding the word of God in prayer. When it is the hardest to pray, it is time to pray the hardest.

Creative Response

In the arms of the pylon opposite we have hidden some tremendous prayer promises directly from his word that our brilliant ancestors prayed throughout history; promises pregnant with power when wielded like a sword and infused with God's power in the face of struggle and pain. Grab one of these for yourself, read it aloud, declare it boldly, and journal or sketch around the pylon image as God reveals more of his epic heart to you.

Meditative Moment

You can not only pray his word but sing it! Go online and find some videos of Sons of Korah and learn a song from Psalms that you can use as a sword.

Take a scripture verse like, "You are the One who saves me. You cover my head in the day of battle" (based on Psalm 140:7), find a common nursery song, or chorus, and sing the words to the tune.

A surrendered prayer Matthew 26:39

A strength prayer Ephesians 3:14-19

A repentance prayer Psalm 51:7, 10-12

The LORD's prayer Matthew 6:9-13

David's prayer Psalm 3

Hannah's prayer 1 Samuel 2:1-10

An enlightenment prayer Colossians 1:9-12

A revival prayer Habakkuk 3:2

Jabez prayer 1 Chronicles 4:10

59

Steely Perseverance

> If my people... will humble themselves and pray... and turn from their wicked ways, then I will hear from heaven, and... heal their land. **2 Chronicles 7:14 (NIV)**

Prayer is powerful because prayer is connection; prayer is relationship with the one who loves us and gave himself for us.

Prayer sets the trajectory of our faith pilgrimage for years to come. The more I engage in all kinds of conversation with my husband, the closer and better I get to know him and the better our marriage gets. So it is in our relationship with God. Building a relationship requires time and patience, which equates to perseverance.

The choices in life that most matter, if we are honest, are not the strategic or functional ones but the relational ones.

The framework of a pylon is constructed from steel. These power structures are built from this material because it is *strong* and is a metal known not to corrode easily in the different seasons of uncertain weather.

If we resolve to devote our hearts to a steely perseverance in the area of prayer we will become strong in heart, and our souls will become like steel in its ability to stand firm and strong even in the most treacherous storms.

Prayer is a shield to the soul, a delight to God, and a terror to Satan. Prayer is powerful and as today's word says, it can "heal lands". It can heal the landscapes of our individual hearts and it can also heal entire nations.

I'm a proud Welsh girl, and just over a hundred years ago in our little nation revival broke out. Over 100,000 people came to know Jesus as Lord and saviour through divine and sacred encounters with Emmanuel. Many tell of generations of people in Wales who committed their way to devoted prayer to see their nation revived. Much of this revival was characterized by the spontaneous prayers of the saints.

Oswald Chambers said this, "The meaning of prayer is that we get hold of God, not of the answer."

I am not saying that prayer is an end in itself, but that prayer is what heals our land; because of God we get to engage in this beautiful, relational conversation. He is the reason, he is the power, he is the source, and if we are engaging with him we can see whole landscapes healed through our steely perseverance in connecting to the king of all kings, who is also the king of our hearts. If we are strangers to prayer, we are strangers to power.

Creative Response

Landscapes are changed through the power of repentance and prayer as today's verse conveys. On the following page, is a map of the UK. Mark a pylon on a region you are committed to pray for. Maybe it's your community, maybe it's the whole country. Bring this place to mind and pray with steely perseverance that God will hear from heaven and heal this land.

Meditative Moment

Picture Jesus looking at the map of the UK. What are his dreams? What are his prayers to the Father? How can you echo him? In what ways has Jesus demonstrated steely perseverance in loving you?

Enormous Ears

> *This is the confidence which we have before him, that, if we ask anything according to his will, he hears us.* **1 John 5:14 (NASB)**

The point of prayer isn't the power that it releases, but the person it reveals. Jesus is known for his enormous heart. His enormous arms stretch as wide as the whole world. His enormous love *never* runs out and the above verse reminds me of his enormous ears. Not literally, of course, but his amazing ability to hear from heaven *all* our prayers.

When we pray, we are caught up in someone bigger than we have ever known. Our words *never* fall on deaf ears, but stand like wired pylons across the landscape of our God's eardrums – always heard, never forgotten. Offering our prayers to God isn't about the answer we may or may not receive, but the beautiful connectedness to the Lord of all creation. How much more then should we desire these spiritual "enormous ears" for ourselves? So that as he constantly listens to us, and as we wait for his response, we close our ears to voices of compromise and make ourselves pylons of truth that champion *his* will and *his* yes and no answers to our prayers as the absolute best way forward for our hearts.

The world is so full of words, but we don't need more noise; we need our ears to be open to the deep stillness of his presence. I love the verse that says, "You have made known to me the paths of life; you will fill me with joy in your presence" (Acts 2:28, NIV).

He hears our prayers *always*, and his will for us in answering these prayers is always to lead us to his path of life. God answers our prayers in one of three ways: yes, no, or wait. He is with us in our prayers (Matthew 28:20). He provides a way out of every trial we pray about.

The point of prayer is not the power it releases but the person it reveals (1 Corinthians 10:13). Nothing is beyond the reach of prayer.

Creative Response

Write your prayers out on the wires of the pylons opposite and then speak them out loud. Let the sound waves of your prayers rise to heaven and know that your heavenly Father is in the room and you have his full attention.

Meditative Moment

"Always heard, never forgotten." If you truly believed that, how large would you pray?

"His delays are not denials." Have you grown weary of unanswered prayer and stopped persevering? Confess it to Jesus.

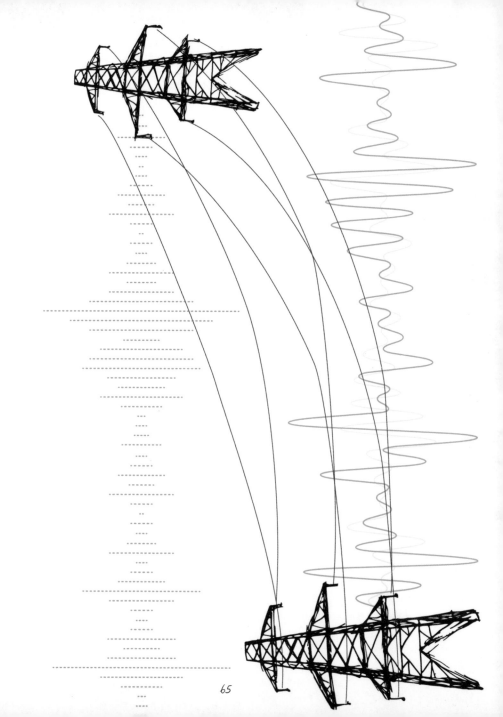

The Prize is Worth the Price

If we want to stand stronger in faith than ever before, we must first sink to our knees, or whatever posture helps us best receive his love.

Prayer requires our time and attention, but we find that the cause is worth the cost if we give space for a prayerful posture.

Prayer literally slaps handcuffs on the enemy's handiwork. In seasons when my anxiety disorder has been raging like a roaring monster, I have found that when I align my heart to pray in the midst of the battle, I am taken out of every domain of the enemy and into the unbeatable presence of my God.

John Piper once said, "Prayer is the Christian's most glorious privilege, most enlarging opportunity and most essential obligation: for prayer opens the door to communication with God himself."[3]

There is such pressure on our time in today's society, but we forget that hurry is the enemy of intimacy. As his sons and daughters, we can so easily get absorbed in these attitudes and time restraints.

Pylon People are a praying people who root down their knees in the muddy landscapes: surrendered, not striving; presence filled, not professional; devoted, not dutiful. As we get low, the world thinks we are naive and so small and timid, but in eternity's economy we become the tallest "spiritually", gaining panoramic perspectives of the "higher thoughts and ways" much like the physical pylons we see dotted at every juncture.

Are we willing to pray the price and gain the greatest prize our hearts and lives have ever known? For me this has been a journey of devoted, continuous prayer that steers me away from sleepy complacency and wakes me up to the knowledge of his glory. For the earth is filled with the knowledge of the glory of God. He's everywhere and prayer keeps us awake to this knowledge. The price to pray is worth every bit of cost.

---

3   John Piper, *A Hunger for God* (Wheaton, IL: Crossway Books, 1997).

Creative Response

Reflect over the past ten days. Use the pylons on the next page to connect and express your revelations from each day in words, images, collaging. Think seriously about some of the questions you have; ask the Holy Spirit to fill in the gaps. We are all on a journey and he has *all* the answers.

Meditative Moment

Where have you seen in your life, in art, music, or any human endeavour the prize being worth the price? What might the price be for you to be steered away from sleepy complacency to a knowledge of his glory?

PART THREE

Pylon People are Perspective People

Scripture tells us that he is "the way and the truth and the life" (John 14:6, NIV). Pylon People are those who recognize his guidance as the ultimate perspective.

- Without *his way* there's no real destination of value.
- Without *his truth* there's no knowing that lasts.
- Without *his life* there's no living in true abundance.

Over the next ten days we will explore how God-given perspectives can change the trajectory of our hearts to an upward gaze: the higher perspective. Pylons stand tall, stand high; their perspectives are both rooted in the reality of earth, yet stretch up to heavenly heights. May we be people who run into the darkness, standing between heaven and earth with fire from the altar (God's spirit) and incense (the prayers of the saints).

New Mind Skins

> *Let God transform you into a new person by changing the way you think.* **Romans 12:2 (NLT)**

In order to live to the fullest – our God-given destiny – we have to "set our minds" on the right things. The poet Frederick Langbridge once wrote about two men who looked out through the same prison bars. When asked what they saw, one said "mud" and the other said "stars". Both men had identical circumstances but entirely different perspectives.

Pylon People, much like the steely pylons, are rooted in earth but they have the *high view*. Pylons set in landscapes are circumstantially rooted in the reality of a muddy field, yet their towering heights can allow them to choose the "stars" for their perspective rather than mud.

It's not what you look at that matters, it's what you "see". "Set your mind on things above, not on things on the earth" (Colossians 3:2, NKJV).

Let's be people who live an epic existence, people who habitually see higher and think great thoughts.

You don't need to strive in order to gain these new perspectives; it's all about surrender. It's not about conjuring up great thoughts, but allowing God access to your mind so that he can transform the mundane into the mega, the broken into the brilliant, the lack into liberty... into freedom.

"Those who live in accordance with the spirit have their minds set on what the spirit desires" (Romans 8:5, NIV). If we are willing to give God access to our minds, he *can* and *will* transform our minds according to his spirit at work in us.

Creative Response

Thoughts come and go across our minds like clouds, punctuated by the occasional shaft of sunlight.

In the silence, hear the cloudy perspectives – write them in and around these clouds. Then ask God to come and transform those clouded thoughts into rays of sunshine. Wait in his presence and replace the clouded thoughts with sunny ones – write the sunny mindsets in the space below.

Meditative Moment

Imagine you are one of the priests crossing the River Jordan (Joshua 3:15–16). You put your feet in the muddy deeps. Are you more conscious of the mud between your toes or God beginning to part the water?

Imagine you are the man for whom Jesus mixes spittle and mud and places it on your eyes (John 9:6). Are you repulsed or hopeful?

Remember the Result!

> *In all these things we are more than conquerors through him who loved us.* **Romans 8:37 (NIV)**

It was a sunny February afternoon in Wales. It was as if the whole nation had been caught up in song, and a sea of red swept the nation as the rugby jerseys came out of hiding for another year for the opening game of the Six Nations: Ireland v Wales.

My husband and I are massive Wales rugby fans: proud Welsh folk. This one particular match, my husband was away and so I sat nervously on my own in my front room as Wales played the boys in green.

It was a nail-biting match. The score was so up and down that it was reminiscent of the hilly valleys of deep Wales. There were screams of frustration followed by voices raised in anthemic song, which I could hear not just from my own living room but seeping through the walls of our terraced house as neighbours celebrated the momentous moments, and commiserated the not-so-magnificent ones!

It was seventy-nine minutes in and Ireland were 5 points up on us. "That's it," I thought, "we're doomed." (I did go to acting school so I am rather dramatic at times!) But with just one minute to go, the boys in red grabbed hold of that oval ball and took it home over the try line. We scored a try in the last minute and a conversion in extra time. Wales had won! I was ecstatic and I needed a whisky to calm me down!

My husband was travelling back from a speaking engagement and phoned me on his journey back. Before I could utter a word, he said, "Cath, don't say anything! Not a word! If you even breathe I will know the result, so just keep silent. I want to watch the match as though I am watching it live. Rewind the TV to the first minute and leave it on pause for when I arrive. I'll be back in half an hour and, listen, Cath, I don't want to see your face when I come in, 'cos if I catch a glimpse of your smile or your frown I'll know. You are welcome to watch it with me again but please sit behind me and don't make a sound or I'll know!"

He was very passionate, so like a good wife, I did what he asked. Thirty minutes later he comes through the door with a coat over his head so he ensured he didn't catch a glimpse of any "give-away" expressions.

For the next eighty minutes, I sat behind him and watched the match again. I saw his head through all the highs and all the lows and come to that exact place I did at the seventy-ninth minute. "We're doomed," he said. In all honesty, I was so taken up in the moment that I too got into this way of thinking, and disappointment gripped me for a moment. Then, all of a sudden, I *remembered*! "Hang on," I thought, "I have got a different perspective here. I know the end result, I *know* that we win. I know that Wales are going to conquer Ireland." I was so caught up in the reality of my husband's emotions and the losing reality of those last moments, I had forgotten the bigger picture of the actual result! Wales will win!

I think this is often what happens in life. Fears, circumstances, and disappointments can cloud our vision so dramatically that we forget the *eternal perspective*!

Despite our feelings, the reality is *God has won and we are more than conquerors*! Even in the most difficult, disappointing moments, our salvation is secured and our destiny awaits.

Pylon People are those who pause in his presence to *remember* the reality of the final score. No matter what the "game" looks like at thirty minutes or thirty years or seventy-eight minutes or seventy-eight years, when the whistle blows, he wins. He won, so that's our destiny too, because we are on his team! Let's fight for the perspective of "conqueror" even in the midst of the days when it feels like we are losing.

Creative Response

On the opposite page, remember what God has done. Remember your eternal reality in Christ. The trophy is ours. Opposite, in the "trophy cupboard" take some moments to *remember* what God has won for us and for *you*. Label the trophies with words like "salvation" followed by the date you were saved, or even more personal memories where God came through and WON for you. The reality is this trophy cupboard will just grow and grow as we keep living in the beauty of the "winning side".

Meditative Moment

When was the last time you forgot God's faithfulness to complete all that concerns you? Sing "Great is Thy Faithfulness" as slowly as possible and remember his goodness.

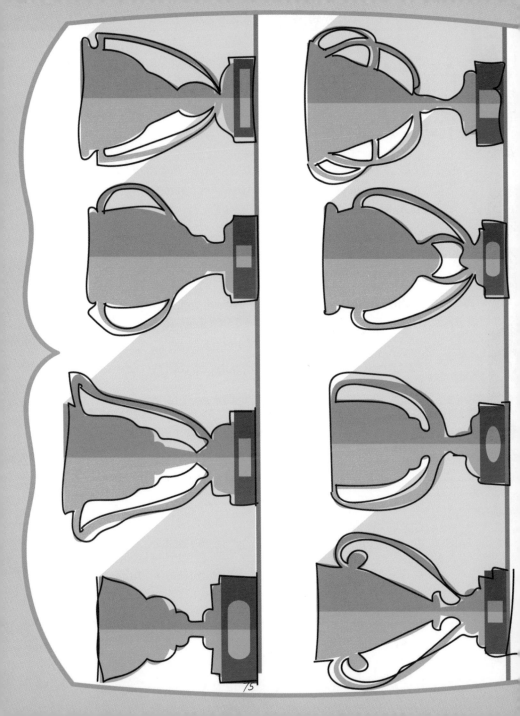

Muddy Puddles or Gushy Fountains?

> Look...! Observe! Be astonished! Wonder! Because I am doing
> something in your days – you would not believe if you were told.
> **Habakkuk 1:5 (NASB)**

Don't fall for the enemy's illusions that keep our minds locked downward.
Abolish the muddy puddle and replace it with the gushing, living fountain.
Here's a poem for you to consider:

Muddy puddles. Head in the brown black.
Time travel in reverse as each tick tock gets slowly drowned
in selfish muddy puddles.

Head down with sort of reflections of this face distorted in the
brown, tired water.
Reflections... deeper reflections of ego, fantasies of my
control.
A bitter un-freedom as I become locked in the downward
gaze.

The self-indulgent spirituality of muddy puddle faith.

Or

Gushy-fountain feasting.
One of brimming joy in light of spring of life.

Gushy-fountain living welcomes cleansing and feasting.

Because despite my sinning...
His smile and endless grinning is unstoppable affection.

Gushy-fountain cleansing wakes me back to life and sends
   my soul to spinning.
I will feast on this fountain gush and this is where I'm
winning.

Eyes off muddy-puddle-muddled me and onto the living king
   where gushy fountains of living water flow from his mouth.

You see

Muddy-puddle gazing locks me in mere mortal lazing,
Whereas gushy-fountain feasting partners me with his divine-
   destiny reaching.
Muddy puddles, dirty pools of dormant water.

There is no movement here.

A small area of collected liquid left from rainstorms now
   passed.
I'm reminiscing over old material where my soul says it's
   time to move on.

But

Fulsome gushy-fountain freedom...
A body of pulsing water that flows and moves.

Renews and broods with every single gushing exclamation.
An overly enthusiastic, lavish, unrestrained expression of
   exuberant abundance.
Life-full.
Soul-full.
Heart-full.
O gushy fountain of living water.
I chose you.

Creative Response

As Pylon People, we don't want to have "head-down" spirituality but a "lifted gaze". These are Pylon People perspectives. We don't want to settle for the reflection of pylon existence in the face of a puddle, but live in the fullness of the pylon perspectives we get as we say no to complacent reflections and run after the real deal! In the poem illustration below, doodle or write your reflections on your own muddy-puddle muddles and gushy-fountain goodness. Write a psalm of your collected thoughts.

Meditative Moment

Like muddy puddles, we can gaze at our own wounds, or gaze at the wounds of Christ. How might Jesus want to lift your gaze in this season? Take a moment to gaze on him. Describe what it would be like to experience God's "unstoppable affection waking you to life".

The Occupied Throne

> *Let us then approach God's throne of grace with confidence, so that we may receive mercy and find grace to help us in our time of need.* **Hebrews 4:16 (NIV)**

Pylon People stand in the immovable perspective that God's throne is *always* occupied. He is in that seat and no one will trick him out of it. God isn't leaving the throne. He rules and loves, and as much as Satan covets that seat, it belongs to our God who occupies it day and night. Nothing can thwart his reign.

On a daily basis, I sit in many a seat. Office chairs, comfy sofas, kitchen stools, cosy bean bags – jumping from one space to the next, constantly distracted by the demands of the day.

I am a "busy bee" sort of girl and echoes of my mam and dad's pleas to "sit still" now come from my husband! Sometimes I'm sitting working in my office and he comes in with a cup of tea, greets me with a kiss, and leaves to go and do his own thing. I decide I need a change of scenery so head downstairs to work in the living room. My husband decides he needs to ask me a question, so he comes to the office and I'm not there. He finds me downstairs.

We have a conversation and he heads back to his space. By now I'm getting a bit hot and bothered, so decide to head out into the garden with a homemade smoothie and work from the deck overlooking our lovely Welsh countryside.

My husband is inside, making his way downstairs to engage in conversation with me and, again, he finds I'm not there. He looks in every room and can't find me and slowly gets more agitated in his desire to get an answer. This is often the case in our home and, upon finding me in the Welsh sun, for the umpteenth time, I hear the words tumble from his mouth, "Cath, I wish you would sit still!"

This is the opposite to the immovable stance of our God. He is undistracted in his love toward us and his throne is continually occupied as he pursues us in every moment!

I bless you to know that his throne will never be empty. His throne is only and always full as he longs more than anything to engage with us – his children – as often as we are willing.

I bless you to know that every moment you can approach God's throne of grace with confidence, finding exactly what you need.

I bless you to find his undistracted gaze and his beautiful mercy and grace for every season. You'll never find Jesus playing musical chairs. He is installed on his heavenly throne to rule with love and power and justice, and *nothing* or *no one* will move him from reigning.

Creative Response

Sit. Find a chair right now. I dare you to just sit in that one place for fifteen minutes (set an alarm). No instructions. Don't do anything. Just be. Think about this phrase only – "The Occupied Throne" – as you occupy that seat. Ask the Holy Spirit to reveal in the stillness the reality of what the occupied throne means for your life in him. After these moments, write down your revelations above the picture of the stool opposite. Be amazed at the power of the "occupied throne" perspective.

Meditative Moment

When it feels like God is playing musical chairs, what one thing from this meditation will you remember?

God-Enthroned, be revealed in splendour as you ride upon the cherubim! How perfectly you lead us, a people set free. Loving shepherd of Israel – listen to our hearts' cry! Shine forth from your throne of dazzling light. **Psalm 80:1 (TPT)**

Won

> *The faithful love of the Lord never ends! His mercies never cease.*
> **Lamentations 3:22 (NLT)**

Salvation is not an on and off phenomenon. Through Christ the reality is we aren't on the "winning side"; we are on the side that *has won*. Jesus' death *has* won our salvation *every day*, never ceasing, never ending. Oh, what a saviour!

Where there is no assurance of salvation, there is no peace – no peace equals no joy and no joy results in fear-based lives! This is not the perspective we should live under. God has **won** today and every day. As Pylon People, we need to live in the assurance of this perspective.

God's hold on us is assured. We can trust his hold on us more than our hold on him! How thankful I am for this reality!

His faithfulness isn't dependent on yours. His love isn't contingent upon our performance. Don't measure your life by your ability – measure it by God's!

God's love does not and will not end. If you have received Christ as Lord and saviour, having repented of your sins, you have *won*.

Let your eyes be still and your hands be free as you contemplate this beautiful, extraordinary perspective. *You have won because he has won.*

Let this perspective fill *all* your vision and take your empty hands into the hands of the king, allowing his power to flow forth into you. *He has won! Hallelujah!*

Creative Response

Around the sketchnoted word "won", on the following page, create a "word map" of everything this means for you as a daughter or son of God. Allow this perspective to bowl you over. As you sketchnote these words of truth, play or sing a song of praise as you come into the *higher* perspective of the *won* way.

Meditative Moment

Reflect on the verse "The Lord sees not as man sees: man looks on the outward appearance, but the Lord looks on the heart" (1 Samuel 16:7, ESV).

Meditate on how the world's values are totally different to kingdom values. Repeat this line as a prayer: "Your kingdom come, in my perspectives, as it is in heaven." Amen.

Famous Last Words

> *So when Jesus had received the sour wine, he said, "It is finished!"*
> *And bowing his head, he gave up his spirit.* **John 19:30 (NKJV)**

She sits on the floor of this dusty, shabby cell, awaiting her final moments. The footsteps of her executioner reverberate around the stone walls of the corridor outside. She sits – afraid – uncertain of the atrocities to come. Head between her knees she is scared to look up as the door creaks open. She daren't lift her head as he begins to speak. She has played this moment over and over in her mind for years, she knows what he must say; "It's time, time to pay for your mess."

But she hears something completely different: "You are free to go – they took Jesus instead of you."

The door swings fully open; freedom awaits her. "This can't be right," she thinks.

Her thoughts tumble about in a million different directions. The guard barks at her, "Get out!" She runs to the door and there awaiting her, just around the corner, she finds herself in the light of a new dawn, perfectly pardoned...

She is overwhelmed, in disbelief at this miraculous turnaround of events. She mutters under her breath quietly to herself over and over, "What just happened?"

She hears a sure voice rise up from within and outside of her, "It is finished". That's what happened!

It is the voice of her saviour, bearing the weight of all wrong upon his shoulders. His famous last words become the beginning words of grace for all humanity: the only last words ever uttered that are anything but an ending, but rather mankind's new beginning. Famous last words becoming freedom's forever fanfare.

What just happened? Grace is what happened!

Creative Response

God is constantly in the business of recycling the old into something new. He takes the mess and makes it into a message of grace. Think about some of your messes, things you think are past repair. Take them through the diagram below and find his famous last words becoming your new beginning.

Meditative Moment

Sit in a quiet room and contemplate yourself in a cell with all the fears and shame that hold you back. Picture these feelings as pieces of furniture crowding the room you are in. The door opens and you are greeted by a guard. He holds the door wide and welcomes you to exit the room. You walk out of the claustrophobic atmosphere into the vast spaces of freedom. The guard locks the door behind you and throws the key into the ocean that lies on the other side of the cell. Recognize that the old has gone and the new has begun. Your fears have been replaced with freedom – it was Jesus who came to set you free and threw away the key to your sin and shame. Now thank him for what this means to you. Let gratitude overflow.

clean slate

IT IS FINISHED

new start

Rooting and Reaching

And after you have done everything, to STAND.
Ephesians 6:13 (NIV, emphasis mine)

Every year since 2014 I have had the privilege of co-leading a worship conference in Singapore. Worshipping God with 8,000 of the saints from around the globe has always been a highlight of mine.

One thing that struck me the first time I visited, and ever since, was the trees – trees so tall I wondered how they even managed to hold themselves up! Just staring up at them in my vertically challenged frame made me feel like I was going to topple over.

One day while looking out my hotel window, I took the picture opposite. Tall trees standing by a pool of water.

The trees were so tall it was like they were holding a conversation with both heaven and earth at the same time. These trees were deliberately rooted in the soil, deeply rooted, but they were also reaching up, reaching high beyond their surroundings.

I want to be like these trees. Remaining *rooted* in Christ's finished work. Rooted in who *he* is, and rooted in his divine truth. Rooted in his love, which loves me as much on my worse day as my best.

I also want to be *reaching*. Reaching for the higher perspectives. Reaching out to all in need – the poor, the lost, everyone and anyone. Reaching deep into my pockets to feed the hungry and give abundantly. Reaching wide, with arms wide open to all who come my way – sharing the love of Jesus and the good news of the gospel at every opportunity.

I don't want to be satisfied with just *rooting* – here I could become so insular and isolated. In the same vein, I don't want to be just *reaching* – this would leave me feeling worn out. I want to do both – *root* deep in Christ and *reach* out in love.

Pylons *stand* in their surroundings – rooted in earth yet reaching out.

Let's be people who *root* and *reach*, who *stand* unhindered in our saviour.

I want to be like the Singaporean trees – *rooted* and *reaching*. To stand, planted by streams of living water.

REACHING

ROOTED

Creative Response

In the space below add your own doodles, sketches, and words exploring how you can *root* more in Christ in the bottom half of the space and how you can actively *reach* more in the top half.

Meditative Moment

Reflect on the truth that as a son or daughter of God you are *rooted* in his love every moment... You are *anchored* in him.

Then reflect on the *reaching* arms of your heavenly Father, which are always open. You are *surrounded* by him. What does it mean to be *anchored* and *surrounded* by a God who never leaves you? This is your reality in Christ – *this is your standing.*

Inside Out

Who believes what we've heard and seen?
Who would have thought God's saving power would look like this?

The servant grew up before God – a scrawny seedling,
a scrubby plant in a parched field.

There was nothing attractive about him,
nothing to cause us to take a second look.

He was looked down on and passed over,
a man who suffered, who knew pain firsthand.

One look at him and people turned away.
We looked down on him, thought he was scum.

But the fact is, it was our pains he carried –
our disfigurements, all the things wrong with us.

We thought he brought it on himself,
that God was punishing him for his own failures.

But it was our sins that did that to him,
that ripped and tore and crushed him – our sins!

He took the punishment, and that made us whole.
Through his bruises we get healed.
Isaiah 53:1–5 (MSG)

Our perspectives should look so different to that of the world. Just yesterday, as I travelled from west to east Wales, I must have seen a hundred or so pylons dotting the landscape. In many ways these odd looking structures are eyesores, yet their significance in the power they carry is what feeds thousands of homes here in the UK. These pylons, somewhat ugly in their appearance, made me think of the cross of my saviour.

Outwardly you see a pain-racked Jesus, a victim in agony and weakness, powerless sympathizers at his feet, mocking voices rattling insults. But take a deeper look. If he wanted, in a flash he could have summoned thousands of angels to annihilate his murderers. Just one release of his concealed power could have swept down from that cross and obliterated his enemies.

That which "looks" like weakness in its most agonizing form is in actuality love stronger than death. The outward expression of "dying" looks to accentuate the reality of his undying love for generations

This is the sublime paradox of the cross of Christ – love's victory! Outwardly we see the deep tragedy of sin: inwardly we see the highest triumph of divine grace. Outwardly we see a miscarriage of justice: inwardly we see the sovereignty of the divine purpose of God to save mankind. Outwardly we see what looks like the powers of darkness overruling and winning: inwardly we see the very opposite at hand.

The cross of cruel catastrophe becomes mankind's magnificent magnet in drawing all men and women to a God we would otherwise be unable to touch. Let's gain God's perspective – looking beyond what is seen to the deep secrets of the unseen. Pylon People are people of divine perspectives!

Creative Response

Below is a hand-drawn landscape of a pylon and the cross: two structures misunderstood. Picture yourself as the pylon.

On the electricity cables that connect the pylon and the cross, write some "outward" statements of your own, letting the sentence change its trajectory to the "inward" reality of what the cross has won for *your* heart.

Write the "outward" statements in black and then change to coloured pens for the "inward" truth!

Meditative Moment

Meditate on the image – listen – what is God saying through it to your heart?

Big Picture Thinking

> *Fixing our eyes on Jesus, the pioneer and perfecter of faith. For the joy set before him he endured the cross, scorning its shame, and sat down at the right hand of the throne of God.*
> **Hebrews 12:2 (NIV)**

Let's keep our eyes focused on the cross today.

Jesus looked beyond the perspective of the revolting torture that was happening to him toward the ultimate triumph of what would be won! It seems impossible, but his crucifixion is in some ways a coronation. A crown of thorns so treacherously bound – yet the deeper situation was that he was being crowned the *ultimate* king of love. To the redeemed those painstaking thorns were becoming eternal diadems, and these wounds were the richest of jewels! This redeeming love not only transforms this ugly picture from crucifixion to coronation but the cross becomes the highest throne. What a saviour!

There may be some places in your life right now that are so painful. It's hard to see any horizon as you are knee-deep in the valley. Jesus died so that we can maintain a perspective beyond our circumstances. The thorny reality of your pain can become the most beautiful of crowns. All things work together for good to those who love the Lord. Endure in love and perseverance.

Take a beat. Thank God for the cross. See the realities of such tribulation becoming the ultimate triumph.

- Crucifixion to Coronation.
- Tribulation to Triumph.
- Weakness to Wedding preparations.
- Sadness to Salvation.

Creative Response

On the next page is a sketch of the crown of thorns interspersed with intricate diamonds.

Above I started to play with alliterated paradoxical short phrases, symbolizing both the agony and the abundance found at the cross. Weave your own alliterated sentences into the art along one of the thorns that leads to a diamond. Try to think of as many as you can. Weave these statements into the image – highlight them in yellow to symbolize the light opposing darkness.

Meditative Moment

Ponder these incredible truths:

- Crucifixion to Coronation.
- Tribulation to Triumph.
- Weakness to Wedding preparations.
- Sadness to Salvation.

Allow these divine exchange freedoms to replenish the voice of the accuser in your mind so that the advocate's voice is what defines you.

Distance Defied

> Let us then with confidence draw near to the throne of grace, that we may receive mercy and find grace to help in time of need.
> **Hebrews 4:16 (ESV)**

Here in the UK when travelling on our motorways there are signs dotted along the hard shoulder displaying phrases such as "Keep Your Distance". This is an instruction to keep us safe – always a good thing!

During a trip to London to see some friends I remember about six of these signs grabbing my attention… "Keep Your Distance". It was like a whisper from God reminding me that he would *never* utter these words. In my mind's eye I saw a picture of a new sign being erected upon this journey of faith, one that said *"Distance Defied* – Stay Close". Because of the cross and the resurrected Christ, *all* distance between us and God has been defied. Nearness to the Father is our new standing in Christ.

Creative Response

Skim read through the past ten days. Use the pylons on the next page to connect and express your revelations from each day in words, images, collaging. Think seriously about some of the questions you have; ask the Holy Spirit to fill in the gaps. We are all on a journey and he has *all* the answers.

Meditative Moment

Read the book of Hebrews, specifically the following passages (or just choose one if time is tight): Hebrews 4:16, 7:25, 10:22, 11:6. The theme of this book is "access" to God. Meditate on the truth that you have an access all areas pass to intimate relationship with your Father through the cross of Christ. You can draw *near*. Distance has been defied.

98

PART FOUR

DAYS 31-40

Pylon People are Present People

> *Surrender your anxiety! Be silent and stop your striving and you will see that I am God.*
> *I am the God above all the nations, and I will be exalted throughout the whole earth.* **Psalm 46:10 (TPT)**

Being "present" is more challenging in today's culture, because we have 24/7 exposure to the world, and the world has 24/7 access to us. Because of this I think we miss out on *so* much.

In these final nine days, we will try discover together the beauty of being "present" to a God who is "ever present".

The point of his power is **always** in the present moment. How would our minds and hearts change if we kept thinking of the present moments as the only moments truly available to us and them being the door to all the other moments to come?

Practise Wonder

For the earth will be filled with the knowledge of the glory of the Lord. **Habakkuk 2:14 (NIV)**

We often think that our greatest "abilities" are found in what we do, but I believe that our greatest ability is our *availability* to the God who wants to open our eyes in wide-eyed wonder to all that surrounds us.

Most of us take for granted our senses: hearing, sight, touch, taste, and smell. One of my favourite poets, Gerard Manley Hopkins, had this to say in his 1887 poem "God's Grandeur":

> *The world is charged with the grandeur of God.*
> *It will flame out, like shining from shook foil;*
> *It gathers to a greatness, like the ooze of oil.*

Nature is never spent.

Spend some time in prayer asking God to open up each of your spiritual senses to new revelation. These sounds and sights can draw us beyond ourselves and inspire us to praise and wonder at our creator God. This is what we were made for: "The chief end of man is to glorify God and enjoy him forever" (Westminster Shorter Catechism 1).

Pray this simple prayer based on his word with me now as we embark on this journey of being a "Pylon Present" people – fully engaged in right here and right now.

"I pray that the eyes of my heart be enlightened in order that I would know the hope to which you have called me."
Ephesians 1:18

Amen

Creative Response

Buy or pick a flower. See it with open eyes. Smell it with closed eyes. Feel it with closed eyes. Visualize it with closed eyes. Draw it with open eyes. Think outside the box.

Meditative Moment

Go online and search for "Adagio for Strings" by Samuel Barber. Close your eyes as you play it. Let the Holy Spirit use your ears, eyes, and sanctified imagination to paint a picture in your mind of his choosing.

Take a fruit or a piece of fresh bread and deeply inhale its fragrance. What might that fragrance tell you about God?

Where do you most often sense God's presence? What scents come to mind? How do those scents make known the presence of the divine?

As you take a deep breath through your nose and mouth, what do you smell soulfully that reminds you that you are an expression of God? Let every breath you take today, be a reminder of being more open and alive, to knowing God as real, authentic, and attentive.

See Free

> *One thing I ask... this only do I seek: that I may dwell in the house of the Lord all the days of my life, to GAZE on the beauty of the Lord.* **Psalm 27:4 (NIV, emphasis mine)**

I grew up in a village tucked into a valley of west Wales. Passionately Welsh in all things, we would celebrate the big national days with Welsh cakes, much singing, and dressed in all manner of red, draped with daffodils. March is always significant on the Welsh calendar as its first day is our national day, St David's Day.

When I was about six years old, I started to sing, and during the month of March my infant school would put on lunchtime concerts for parents as we sung Welsh songs in celebration of our nation.

The night before the Wednesday concert, I would be so nervous. My mam and dad would come in my bedroom to tuck me in and encourage me emphatically about how brilliant I would be. I always remember my dad saying in his deep, burly Welsh tones, "Cath, beauty, as soon as you get on that stage tomorrow, don't start a note until you find me in that crowd. I'm there with you, just find my eyes."

The next day, I would nervously make my way up onto the little stage of my school and sift through what seemed like a sea of people. At first all I could see were many unfamiliar faces, but as I scanned diligently... *finally* there they were! *My* mam and dad! Egging me on, full of encouragement and smiles just for me, full of faith and life directed into my heart that enabled me to confidently sing out with gusto.

In these moments, I always remember my dad doing a little "sign language" from the crowd. He'd point to his heart and then hit his back while mouthing, "I've got your back!" I will never forget those moments!

This is a beautiful representation of our heavenly Father in our lives. He is always present, egging us on, beaming out "life" in our direction.

As we stand on each new day's stage it can feel daunting, as initially all we can see is a sea of fear, activity, and unsettling emotions. But if we seek him, we will find him amid the voices vying for our attention. As we find his eyes, we will *see free*. As we catch his eyes, we will know his love that gave up everything for us and we will hear his strong, "I have got your back".

As each new day comes and goes, resolve to find *his* eyes and *see* him and his ways as your present reality. He sees you. He has your back. Just open your eyes to see him. His gaze awaits you. *See free*.

Creative Response

Imagine yourself on the stage of a new day. As you look out, all you see are balloons. Different words are written on them: exams, deadlines, to-do lists, illness, worry, shame. All you can see to begin with are these balloons distracting your view.

In the balloons opposite, write down what is blocking your view today. It can be specific situations, names, words, fears. Then surrender each one in prayer to God.

All of these balloons are what you want to let go of. Take a beat and in your mind's eye, one by one see yourself let them go. *Behold* as each one drifts away. Waiting all along behind the wall of balloons is a God whose gaze is *all* for you, a God who has got your back, a Father who beams love to your heart at every moment. *See free*. Clear the distracted view. *He* is here now, waiting for your eyes.

Meditative Moment

Picture in your mind a common repetitive experience of feeling anxious. See Jesus pointing to his heart, and mouthing to you, "I've got your back." Dwell in that moment. Do something that scares you that might bless someone, and picture Jesus with you smiling from ear to ear.

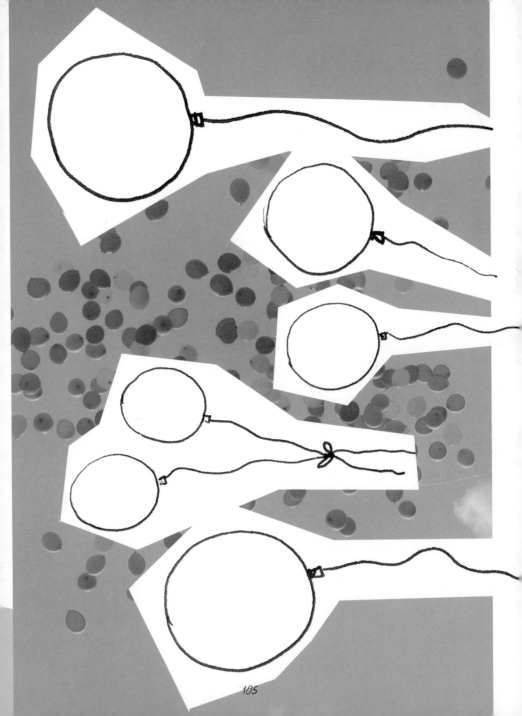

DJ Your Day

> *The Lord your God is with you, the mighty warrior who saves. He will take great delight in you; in his love he will no longer rebuke you, but will rejoice over you with singing.*
> **Zephaniah 3:17 (NIV)**

I remember walking in one of my favourite parts of London, Brick Lane, a few years ago. This place is a heady vibrant mix of colour, art, street food, graffiti – a wonderland of artistry that sets my soul alight.

I walked down this eccentric, creative, urban landscape and wasn't able to click my camera quickly enough to capture all the inspirations that I wanted to stow away.

I was so taken by my surroundings, that I accidentally bumped into a group of people and, as a result, my phone tumbled out of my hand onto the floor. After apologizing profusely, I bent down to pick it up and there written in tiny letters in the corner of the pavement with what looked like a black felt-tip pen was this simple sentence: *Punctuate your days with Hallelujahs.* Amid the decadent art, this one simple graffiti statement caught my heart's attention and everything else faded into insignificance. Isn't it funny that the greatest secrets are often hidden in the most unlikely places? In my excitement I went to the nearest coffee shop and wondered and journaled around this sentence that captivated me deeply. I wanted this to be a personal manifesto for the rest of my days. Over the coming weeks I thought a lot about songs that awakened me to *his* love over recent years. I wanted to open up my ears to hearing truth every day: songs scattered like commas that help me recatch *his* breath through my day. Songs like full stops that remind me to *be* and not *do*. Songs like semicolons that remind me "there's more to come". Hallelujah punctuation marks marking the truth of God in my hearing every day!

Every morning I resolved to listen to the song "Give Me Jesus". Its simple lyrics say, "In the morning when I rise, give me Jesus. You can have all this world, just give me Jesus." In the evenings, I now listen to another favourite of mine, "The Peace" by Graham Kendrick, a song that reminds me that in the night his song is over me.

This simple graffiti also compelled me to create song lists in my iPhone: folders of Hallelujah punctuation at the ready for moments when I need a truth reboot. I have one playlist labelled "Valley" for when life gets tough. This playlist is full of songs that speak hope into the hopeless. Another playlist is called "Praise" and is full of declarations of the greatness of my God. Another is called "Battle" for when life throws a curveball and includes songs that remind me that "If God is for us, who can ever be against us", Romans 8:31 (NLT).

Why not try being present in your hearing of his truth by punctuating your day with hallelujahs? Fill your ears with *his* truth. In the same way he loved us first, he sings over us first. He rejoices over you with singing. Tune in. Listen. His song is the truest song you will ever hear and nothing can silence it. Be the DJ of your day and punctuate your hearing with hallelujahs that bring you present into his truth.

Creative Response

Creatively design your three favourite lyrics on the manuscript on the next page. Then where there is a full stop, a comma, and a semicolon, think about songs you can punctuate your day with that will accentuate the presence of *his voice* ringing in your ears. Remember he is your advocate, not an accuser.

Meditative Moment

Imagine you're in a concert where Jesus is the main attraction, and he stops and sings a song just for you. What is he singing?
Try breathing in with "Hal", pause and hold your breath, and think "lelu" and exhale the name of God, "Jah". Let his praise calm you.

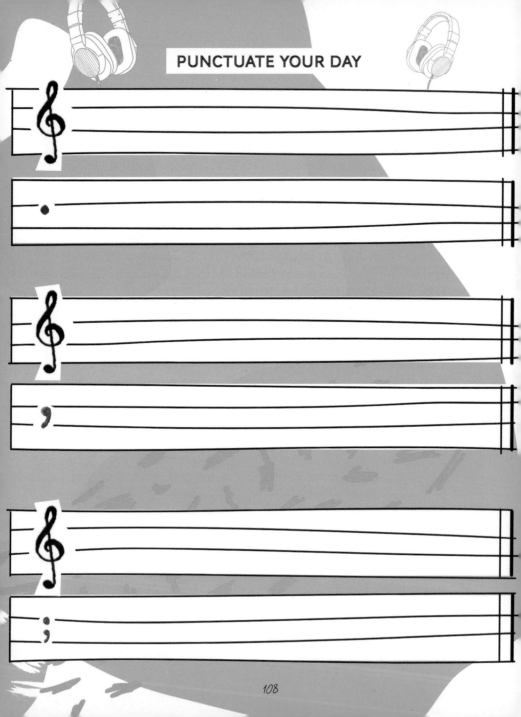

Can't Touch This

> *Then the Lord reached out his hand and touched my mouth and said to me, "I have put my words in your mouth."*
> **Jeremiah 1:9 (NIV)**

One of the senses we maybe don't talk about as often as we should is touch. Dotted throughout the word of God are glimpses of the touch of God upon his people. We read above in Jeremiah about how one touch from God put words in Jeremiah's mouth.

Psalm 104 talks about God touching the mountains and how they shake as a result. In the Gospels, we see Jesus touch people suffering from leprosy and see them cleansed and healed. It's almost like the touch of God releases unfathomable power. Jesus is the touchable Christ. I remember a song that we used to sing that said, "Just one touch from the king changes everything." I'm also reminded of the woman in Matthew 9 who thinks, "If I can just touch the hem of his garment, I will be healed." In faith she pursues this life-hanging touch and walks away in complete freedom.

I remember at the beginning of this journey trying to travel in an attitude of "practising wonder". I felt more disengaged from touch than any of the other senses. I prayed into this and one day I travelled to Porthcawl on the south coast of Wales. As I sat gazing out to sea, I was unconsciously running the sand beneath me through my hands. Its touch was warm and soft and I was drawn to what it felt like to touch.

I remembered that beautiful verse in Psalm 139:17–18: "My thoughts for you outnumber the grains of sand on the earth." As I felt the sand slide through my fingers, unable to calculate the thousands of grains, I became overwhelmed with gratitude as I recognized that the thoughts of the God of creation are toward little "me".

I sat there that day and wept with joy in a moment of encounter with my saviour. How many more grains of sand are on earth? This is how many thoughts of love and grace and affirmation and mercy he says he has toward us.

This was a moment of experiencing the sensation of touch that led me to encounter the very present presence of my living papa.

O Lord, open up our sense of touch to know you more and to feel your grace, which abounds toward us in every waking moment.

Creative Response

Get outside into wide-open spaces and find a leaf. Stick it in the frame opposite. Leaves are great for "touch". Hidden within them are holes, veins, and bumps. Feel the sensation of the leaf in your hand before you place it in the frame. Be still before God and ask him to open up your sense of touch to encounter what he may be saying to you in this *now* moment.

Meditative Moment

Run your hand across something with texture, and let it remind you of truth. For example, running your hand across an orange or tangerine might remind you that beautiful things are sometimes bumpy and rough. Feel the wind across your face. What wisdom can you hear?

PLACE YOUR LEAF HERE

Scentsation

> *Our lives are a Christ-like fragrance rising up to God.*
> **2 Corinthians 2:15 (NLT)**

I have never outgrown my delight in my favourite aromas! Smelling coffee brewing first thing in the morning; chocolate in Bruges; the unbeatable scent of fresh bread; newly cut grass in summertime. Divine!

Wherever I am, there is something about these earthly aromas that make me come alive. As I breathe them in, different memories come flooding back of times passed; brilliant memories made.

There is something about this sense of smell that awakens me to an expanded world. It's as though all the senses broaden the depth and texture of life. When I am fully awake to my senses, they act as beautiful invitations to moments activated more fully. I'm invited to live more engaged with all the beauty, joy, and suffering that is ever present. This is how I long to live. Open to the divine. Awake to the fragrance of Christ.

The activity of opening up our hearts to wonder effuses in itself a trail of the most luxurious "divine perfume", which is the presence of God being more recognized in us. We often smell something before we see it. We can't *see* smells but we *know* they are there. Engaging with aromas that attract me helps my spirit remember and better understand the journey of "we walk by faith, not by sight" (2 Corinthians 5:7, NKJV).

I'm not saying that we physically smell an aroma of his spirit but rather it's as though the divine perfume is an irresistible and inescapable attraction to our encounter with God. We are attracted to his aroma of grace. We long to know and belong with God, real, authentic, and attentively. We experience his presence as though he is an incredible aroma, like morning coffee, the ocean breeze, fresh flowers.

The divine perfume is Christ in us. His divine love, which is incomparable. His grace is so strong no smell could oust it. The fragrance of Christ is both beautiful and powerful, just like when I hug my mam and she is wearing Coco Chanel. As you recognize the aromas that provoke you to wonder, *thank* God for the aroma of his unrelenting love. Ask that this aroma be caught by us and spread like wildfire to generations.

Creative Response

Memories, imagination, old sentiments, and associations are more readily reached through the sense of smell than through most other channels.

Take a moment and think about your favourite smell, or ask God to remind you of a smell that will recall something that captures your heart for him.

Capture this scent if you can. Dab a drop of perfume or laundry detergent, a sprinkle of dirt, or a dab of cinnamon, or anything else on the dots on the following page. How does this scent make you feel? How does it point you to the aroma of Christ? Write your thoughts around the scent.

Meditative Moment

Have you ever encountered someone wearing a strong scent, and the smell lingered after they left the room? What would it be like if you were to be fragrant with Jesus? What would linger in the room? How can the aroma of the Christ you carry provoke people to remember how richly they were loved in your presence?

Deposit
scent
here →

write
↑
← thoughts →
here
↓ ↓

Donut Dive

> *Taste and see that the Lord is good.*
> **Psalm 34:8 (NIV)**

Jesus is the bread of life. He is also described as the "living water". Take a moment to thank God for the hearty taste of salvation and new life.

In the Psalm above, David is inviting us to experience what he has experienced in discovering the goodness of the salvation of his God.

It's almost like David is enticing future generations, almost saying, "Try it – you will like it."

Psalm 34 is a song of gratitude we can all sing when God brings us out of a dark situation. But David's joy is only a foretaste of the future redemption God will bring to all who trust in him through the life, death, and resurrection of Jesus.

I *love* donuts! Especially chocolate ring donuts topped with sprinkles. Even more when they are fresh out the oven, hot and doused in sugar – an impeccable party for my taste buds!

I love the smell of sweet beauty they exude, but the true satisfaction is gobbling this dreamy donut up. If I just looked at the beauty of this marvellous manna or just took in the smell without taking a donut dive, I would miss out on *so much*! The same is true of our God and his word.

Scripture says, "Man shall not live on bread alone, but on every word that comes from the mouth of God" (Matthew 4:4, NIV). Let me tell you, the words of God are the best-tasting donut we will ever eat!

Just as we need nourishment for our bodies from food, we need nourishment for our souls from God. Pursuing God will make your mouth water for more and desire to taste it all – the rich and savoury, the tart and bitter, the sweet and sour.

Let's resolve every day to take an intentional "donut dive", savouring the taste.

Spiritual hunger longs for rich, substantial nourishment, which is served up in the three-course meal of his word.

Creative Response

Take time to think about some key "donut dive" declarations you can learn and cling to. Make one your "Life Verse" manifesto and make the other your "Battle Verse" manifesto. In and around the ring donuts opposite write these verses. Write creatively and learn these spirit-filled scriptures so you can let them roll off your tongue in moments when you need a "donut dive". Put them in you – eat them up, don't just look at them. I find writing Scripture creatively a good way to help me memorize it. Have a go. *Taste and see!*

Meditative Moment

Choose your "Life Verse" manifesto and your "Battle Verse" manifesto from anywhere in Scripture. Repeat them out loud three times, emphasizing the words that are important to you.

Engage in a physical prayer around these verses:

• Surrender – arms up
• Receive – hands out
• Give away – arms out in front of you
• Arms stretched wide – arms wide open

Ask your heavenly Father to help you engage with these physical elements of prayer around your two chosen verses.

life verse

battle manifesto

Welcome Home Banners

> *One thing I ask... this only do I seek: that I may dwell in the house of the Lord all the days of my life, to gaze on the beauty of the Lord and to seek him in his temple.* **Psalm 27:4 (NIV)**

I wonder where you feel most at home? What feelings are conjured up by that place? If you haven't already realized it by now, I am a rather passionate Welsh lady! One of the most magical "coming home" feelings I get is when I cross the Severn Bridge from England into my homeland of Wales.

My husband and I have many a tradition when we cross this precious threshold. As soon as we pass the "Welcome to Wales" sign, we start singing the Welsh national anthem at the top of our voices! We deafen one another and open all the car windows in the middle of the motorway in hope that we will deafen all the other drivers too. After the anthem we put on our "Wales Playlist" and spend the next half hour until we arrive at our house singing, laughing, and enjoying this moment of a deep satisfied "I'm home".

As great as those moments are they soon pass, but the truth is his presence is the *best* home we will ever find. Being with God in his wrap-around embrace, awake to his surround-sound love, and present to his gaze is the most soul-satisfying home we will ever find.

We were made for conscious, continual communion with our God. Consider this poem I wrote:

> *Not to go left where nothing's right.*
> *Or to the right where nothing's left.*
> *But to the place I'm called to be.*

The place of dwelling.
This place of rest.
My home is where I can find my heart.
And my heart is where he is.

One of the names of God is "I am". This in itself shows us him as the *ever*-present God. Let's be awake to I am. He is *home*. Let your heart find home at its very best... in Christ.

Creative Response

Let the words of the poem inspire you. Around "I Am", on the following page, sketch what being *home* in Jesus means to you.

Meditative Moment

Ponder the poem.
Picture yourself in a place your heart identifies as a place of "rest".
How is this place reminiscent of who God is, and how does it reflect him as "home"?

Not to go left where nothing's right.
Or to the right where nothing's left.
But to the place I'm called to be.

The place of dwelling.
This place of rest.
My home is where I can find my heart.
And my heart is where he is.

I AM

(home)

Perceive Before Receive

> *See, I am doing a new thing!... do you not PERCEIVE it? I am making a way in the wilderness and streams in the wasteland.*
> **Isaiah 43:19 (NIV, emphasis mine)**

I have read this part of scripture so many times. It's one of my "Life Verses" – it bellows truth and hope into hopelessness and brings so much life.

This morning as I picked up my Bible, I decided to turn again to this passage. I had a simple personal revelation. It was as I thought in more detail of the word *perceive*. Perceiving is understanding something in our consciousness before it becomes reality. In essence, perceiving is faith.

Here Isaiah is penning the hope of the "new" and asking us, "Do you see it in faith even if you don't see it in reality yet?" It demands faith and zeal. His word says, "We live by faith, not by sight", 2 Corinthians 5:7 (NIV).

In another verse we hear, "What is seen is temporary, but what is unseen is eternal" (2 Corinthians 4:18, NIV) which is all about us being awake to his spiritual dimension. Just as we saw on day 13 – Climb High – his ways and thoughts are higher than ours. Being a Pylon "Present" Person can be a hard thing to navigate when we also need to be perceiving, standing *in* faith for what is yet to come. This is where trust comes in. We can be fully present and trust that God (with *his* higher ways and thoughts) *is* doing a new thing. He *is* making a way in the wilderness. He *is* bringing us streams of life in the wasteland. We can trust that he is doing this *because* his perspective is always higher and further than ours. He is in constant *perceive* mode, so we can rest and *receive*.

Creative Response

Faith (perceiving) is a gift that we can ask for as well as something we already have (1 Corinthians 12).

Spend some time talking to God. Maybe you want to go back to your high place that you visited on day 13? Ask him in which areas of your life he is doing a new thing. Ask him for a gift of faith to perceive what he is doing now. In the illustration opposite of the "stream in the wasteland" and "pathway in the wilderness" write, draw, or sketch the things he shows you. Make a choice today to *perceive then receive*. He is doing a *new thing*. He is a creative God and is always doing a new thing.

Meditative Moment

Repeat the creative response but without the sketchnoting. Be still and know that he is God. Perceive and receive in the stillness that is his divine presence.

Glory Explosion

"For I," declares the Lord, "will be a wall of fire around her, and I will be the glory in her midst." **Zechariah 2:5 (NASB)**

This is a poem I wrote one day while walking in my home town of Pontypridd one beautiful spring day. The Welsh birds were tweeting extra melodically (of course!), the daffodils were beginning to bloom in their sunshine splendour, the green grass seemed more green, the wind was constant yet seemed to be conducting nature all around me like an orchestra. There was no cloud in the sky, just deep bright blue. I got out my journal and "glory explosions" started in my soul's deep.

Creative Response

Add your own fireworks around the poem. Annotate the poem. Which words stand out? Highlight them creatively. What images do they stir within you? Draw them – don't be scared, just do it. Pray into this whole concept of his "glory explosions" all around us at all times. Pray and create at the same time in response to one another.

Meditative Moment

Close your eyes and picture a scene of endless, extravagant fireworks in your mind's eye. Ask the Holy Spirit to guide you to identifying different parts of God's character through the colour and form, size and sound of the different fireworks. Thank him for his glory explosions that are a real part of your journey as a son or daughter of the king of kings.

There is Glory exploding all around me.
Dazzling hope.
Wonderment.
Light kicking darkness out.

There is Glory exploding all around me.
Life launching like fireworks.
In and among what looks like grey.

There is Glory exploding all around me.
In all you created.
In all you are.
In the rays of your radiance even in black skies
there is a star to be found.

Expand my God vision, so
your glory explosions are my panorama.

Expound on the intricacies of Glory
all around, so it's your glory I see.

Glory explosions not gory diversions that settle for less, yet strut a
temporary prowess.
Your Glory explosions are the prize.

A wonderland of revealed revelations of grace and love beyond
our comprehension.

The ultimate explosion of Glory summed up in three glory exploding
words:

It Is Finished
My mess for your grace.
My sin for your forgiveness.
My glum for your unrelenting glory.

The great Glory explosion that changed
my destiny from hopeless to hopefull.
And ever since exploding glories explode

in neighbourhoods across the globe because glory
Himself rose again.
So **now** glory can explode inside of me.
Glory can explode inside of you.
Glory explodes all around us... everywhere.

You chose to give up your glory, so we could be part
of the greatest love explosion story.

#ALLGloryToGodintheHighest

Final Reflections

> *Being confident of this, that he who began a good work in you will carry it on to completion until the day of Christ Jesus.*
> **Philippians 1:6 (NIV)**

Together we have journeyed forty days through themes of power, prayer, perspective, and presence. The core values of a Pylon People existence.

Let's take some time to ponder and press into his presence as we reflect on one key moment in each chapter that inspired us to live these powerful, prayerful, eyes-up, presence-filled lives.

Write a short haiku on each of these themes: Power, Prayer, Perspective, Presence. How you will walk out this particular part of your journey of faith from this moment on? Think creatively about how you could include this haiku poem within an image. Think outside the box as to how you can write these haikus and remember them like life manifestos. A haiku is a simple poem using this structure:

Five syllables
Seven syllables
Five syllables

Thank you so much for coming on this journey with me over the last forty days. One of my favourite quotes comes from the inimitable Saint Augustine, who says, "You have made us for yourself, and our heart is restless until it rests in you." I pray that through this time you have come face to face with Emmanuel – the God who is so radically *with us*. I pray that you will have encountered the God whose name is "I Am" for he is so near in every season.

I end this time together the same way we started, with a chunk of the Pylon People creative prose. I hope that these forty days have achieved these truths in your heart – not by might, or by your own strength, but by his spirit.

Pylon People are powered people;
Praying people;
Present people;
Perspective people;
Pregnant-with-passion people;
A population of persons prone to point to papa's path.
Pylon People are not pipe-dream people,
But propel into Promised-Land purpose.
Pylon People are presence-potent people,
Pledging their purpose and potential to pursuing
   the Prince of Peace.
A posture of present,
A posture of all welcome at all times.
Pylon People are a prophetic people,
Promotion perspectives of pauper to princess, poor to prized,
   paralyzed to powerful.
Pylon People are powered people,
Powered by the protagonist of all history and destiny.